Falling Forward

A MAN'S MEMOIR OF DIVORCE

CHRIS EASTERLY

Cover design by Nicole Armstrong

Printed in the United States of America

First Edition, 2014

ISBN-13: 978-0692330296
ISBN-10: 0692330291

For more information, please contact:
fallingforwardbook@gmail.com

CONTENTS

ACKNOWLEDGMENTS

Thank you to Vicki Easterly and Ron Easterly for your unfailing support.

To Maureen A. Taylor, my editor and friend, who helped me see the forest for the trees.

And to everyone else who made this book possible, especially:

Dony Antony, Nicole Armstrong, Lee Barbee, John Bauman, Kathy Lu Palmore Billingsley, Dan Braun, Fran Briggs, Brenda Bush, Jeremy Casper, Eric Comley, Eric De La Rosa, Sean Dillon, Lisa Madrid Duffy, Ellis and Rose Marie Easterly, Jim and Barbara Easterly, Jennifer Lum Haynes, Shay Haynes, Walker Haynes, Hannah Marie Hines, Ariana Jackson, David Jurmain, Shannon and Zachariah Linton, Mary Margaret Martinez, Mike Moehring, Barbara Nicolosi, James Olsen, Andrew Ortwein, Vicki Peterson, Matt Price, Bob Rice, Luke Schelhaas, Justine Schmiesing, Kelly Shipe, Debbie Smith, Dan Steadman, Deborah Tieberg, Jonathan Vermeer, Mike Werb, Eleanor Wiggins, Charlotte Winters, Merry Zimmerman

Thank you all.

Falling Forward

INTRODUCTION

I've written a book I wish didn't exist. Because that might mean my marriage had survived. That, in some alternate reality, my ex-wife and I still live together. She still comes home after work, and we kiss and take the pug for a walk. We still go on evening jogs through our old neighborhood together. Maybe we even have a toddler and we play with her on the carpet and argue over how to discipline her. On Saturday mornings, we still go out for French toast, chorizo scrambled eggs, and mimosas at our favorite diner. We're older but closer, our bond strengthened by more years of the struggles and blessings of a shared life.

But we don't live in that reality.

When I was going through my divorce, I searched for books that would offer advice and hope, affirm what I was going through, and let me know I'd survive it. So I scoured the shelves. But almost all I found were titles like *When He Leaves*, *Runaway Husbands,* and *A Woman's Journey Through Divorce*. I snatched them up and gleaned their insights.

But where were the books written by men? Eventually, I discovered a handful. Some proved helpful, but few spoke to the pain, grief, and anger I struggled with. Instead, the majority covered topics like how to

1

secure the best attorney, keep your financial assets, gain custody of your children, and have great sex again.

Those are all helpful subjects. But *Falling Forward* is a different kind of book. It explores the emotional landscape of a man's divorce, from his wife's affair and the marriage's collapse to his eventual healing.

This book about divorce is written from a male perspective. Still, we're all human, and pain is no respecter of gender. Fortunately, neither is healing. For this reason, I believe both men and women will recognize in these pages the turmoil of their own divorce and their own all-too-familiar questions:

How do you start a whole new life from the ruins of all you've known for so long? How do you handle the shame of those who judge you—quietly or loudly—for your marriage's failure? Will you ever feel normal again?

What crutches pull you through the hard times and what don't? Will you survive the bottomless grief of losing the most important relationship in your life? Of knowing you'll *never* be with your spouse again? How do you handle dating again after years of marriage, especially when you still love your ex?

Whoever the reader, I'm telling my story for one reason: to assure you that you will survive. During my divorce, I never planned to take my life, but there were times I wished life would just end quickly. That's how painful it was. You may be feeling that too. But I suffered through the night and emerged intact, blinking back the sun, scarred but strong. So will you.

"What's lost is nothing to what's found, and all the death that ever was, set next to life, would scarcely fill a cup."

—Frederick Buechner

CHAPTER 1

THE END

In the dream, I press my body against hers. It's not sexual. It's more primal than that. It's the elemental desire to lose, and find, yourself in another person. But as I pull her close, she turns away. And I'm alone. I've lost her.

Suddenly, I wake.

In reality, it's the second morning of our honeymoon. She lies sleeping on her side, inches away, and relief floods my being. I pull her close. She nestles against me. I feel the warmth of her skin. Smell her hair. She's right here. And she will be forever. Or at least for the next six years.

Our marriage died on a Sunday. The morning began with a baptism, the christening of my friend Dan's baby girl. Dan and I had both moved out to Hollywood after college, he from Indiana to pursue acting, me from Kentucky to pursue screenwriting. Like countless dreamers before us, we were two Midwestern boys chasing our childhood visions of working in the movies.

Now here we were, twelve years later, standing beside our wives in Saint Jude's Catholic Church in tony Westlake Village, an hour outside

Los Angeles, as the priest sprinkled water over his daughter's tiny head. The spacious sanctuary was packed. Sun poured through tall windows, soaking the place in light.

After the ceremony, Dan's friends and family made their way to a nearby country club, where we celebrated over roast chicken and Merlot. A crisp breeze blew in off a local pond and the late afternoon sun sank behind the mountains, casting shadows across the suburb.

After a few hours, my wife M and I hugged Dan and his wife goodbye, then made the long drive back to our apartment in San Dimas. The trip home was filled with the light chatter and comfortable silences that come from being married for more than half a decade. By the time we reached our exit, it was dinnertime so we stopped at In-N-Out, our favorite burger joint.

I always enjoyed sitting across from M at a restaurant where I could look at her face. It was all beautiful angles framed by long red hair, so dark it was almost black. When she laughed, her eyes closed and her face lit up. That night was no different.

After dinner, as we walked through the parking lot back to the car, she moved up behind me and wrapped her arms around my chest. "I love you," she said. It was unexpected. The words flooded through me like warm water. Like reassurance. We drove home. As we walked in our apartment, I asked if she wanted to watch a TV show.

"No," she said. "I want to talk."

I always get a sinking feeling when I hear those words. We sat on the couch. Our pug hopped up between us, waddling back and forth. M was silent. Finally, she spoke, four words I never saw coming.

"I had an affair."

My mind went blank, like a satellite signal scrambled in a thunderstorm. M searched my face for a reaction. It was empty, so she continued.

"With Jeff from work."

The dog plopped down between us.

"Why?" I finally asked.

"I don't know," she said, then shared the details, though I didn't ask for them. It happened two months earlier, for most of September. The fling lasted three weeks, but feeling guilty, M cut it off.

But there was more. The affair resulted in a pregnancy. But she had miscarried. She considered never telling me, but said she couldn't keep it a secret any longer.

I grabbed my car keys and walked out. Where had I felt this before?

Have you ever been punched hard in the face?

In high school, my track teammate was practicing his discus throw and didn't see me behind him. He swung around and smashed his elbow in my teeth. The impact bent my braces. Everything went black. I sank to my knees, but two friends grabbed me on either side and propped me up. Stars sparkled in my field of vision. That's kind of how it felt that night as I drove around San Dimas.

It was already close to midnight, but I needed to talk to somebody, somebody other than my wife. My buddy Brett lived nearby. Like Dan, he was married with a baby daughter, but he answered my phone call anyway, and a few minutes later we met in his front yard and I told him about M's affair.

Brett put his hand on my shoulder and said he was sorry. He wanted to pray for me. Standing in his dark yard, we shut our eyes as cars whipped past on the street in front of his duplex. The air was fall-chilly. He asked that God would help me through all that was to come. I don't remember the exact words. I remember that I had a friend when I needed one. Brett would become an invaluable confidante and sounding board in the months to come. But first, I had to face tonight.

After I left Brett's, I drove around a little longer, listening to the dull hum of my tires on the road. Everything was closed: the Del Taco, the CVS pharmacy, the Vons supermarket. The world had shut down.

When I finally walked back in my apartment, M straightened up on the couch, her face worried. "I'm glad you're home," she said. I tossed my keys on the kitchen table and walked down the hall to the bedroom.

I slept in our bed beside her that night—partly out of routine, but partly because I wasn't ready to face the reality that soon I might never sleep beside her again. I dreamed that night, of me holding her, nuzzling my head gently against her neck. The next morning, I woke and turned to see her lying beside me, softly sobbing.

There would be so much to untangle in the coming days. But it would have to wait. Thanksgiving was two days away, and my mother was flying in from Kentucky to celebrate with us. I picked her up from the airport while M went to work at the nearby hospital where she was a staff psychologist. Would I tell my mom about M's confession? Would I be able not to?

A day passed. My mom sensed something was wrong, but didn't mention it. On Thanksgiving eve, M and I went for a drive, leaving Mom alone at our apartment to rest off her jetlag. As we drove, I slammed my fist on the steering wheel.

"You're my *wife*. How could you do this?"

"I'm a terrible person," M said.

She said Jeff had been persistent. He knew she was married, but he didn't care. He flirted with her for months. Pursued her. Made her feel desirable.

That's something she deserved, and something I hadn't been able to give her in recent months because I had been laid low by a severe clinical depression. I thought I had been experiencing some kind of emotional problem I could remedy through ample psychotherapy. But three counselors had failed to put a dent in my chronic sadness. I shuffled through the days just trying not to cry.

So, a few months before her confession, M began to complain there was no passion in our marriage. She was right. By then, the chemical catastrophe in my brain had rendered me essentially bedridden. It's hard to feel like wooing your wife when all you can manage is lying still. M said she didn't know if our marriage was going to survive. I thought that was an outrageous thing to say; if our marriage lacked passion, then we'd simply do the work necessary to get it back, not *quit our marriage.*

I should've seen the signs, of course. The new crimson lace panties dangling from the clothes rack. (We weren't having sex so they weren't to titillate *me.*) The increasing number of nights she "stayed late at work." The fact that she put on makeup and a svelte green dress to "hang out with her friend Kathryn" on the weekend. Still, it had never crossed my mind to cheat on her, so why would I imagine her ever doing the same?

One early autumn evening, without my knowledge, things came to a head. At twilight, M walked over to Holy Name of Mary Catholic Church, a warm stucco structure that stood across the street from our apartment complex. While I stayed home, she went to the sanctuary to talk with the priest Father David.

Sitting in the confessional across from the old man, she admitted her affair and shared that her marriage had been a struggle for too long. By now, it was so painful she'd been begging God for guidance: should she stay married, or leave? She was so desperate that she begged God to speak to her audibly, like the fiery bush spoke to Moses.

The priest listened to her for what could have only been a few minutes. Then he said that maybe it was time to dissolve her marriage. He said this without consulting me. He also counseled her to keep the affair a secret. M took this as her audible word from God. Apparently, it was time to chalk up the last six years to a loss and call it quits. She came home red-eyed and desolate.

That was two months earlier. Now here we were in late November, the awful truth laid bare, stuck in traffic the night before Thanksgiving. When we finally got home, it was dark out. As we walked in, my mom was watching TV in the living room. She sat on the edge of the couch.

"Is everything okay?"

M sat on the floor. I cried. We told my mom about the affair, and she absorbed it dutifully. She thought we were going to reveal that one of us had cancer. Apparently, a simple extramarital affair was something of a relief to her. I sat on the couch beside Mom.

"I'm going to find Jeff's car and slash his tires," I said.

"Well, whatever happens, whether you stay together or not," Mom said, "you're both going to survive this."

We weren't in a festive mood the next day. The last thing on our minds was prepping a feast. So on Thanksgiving Day, the three of us drove to a nearby Bob's Big Boy restaurant. There were only five other people in the whole place. My mom and M ordered the turkey-and-stuffing special. I ate a warmed-over cheeseburger and fries. Everything felt strangely normal. We talked, laughed, cracked jokes.

There was a reason that last holiday lunch didn't turn into a bloodbath: even an extramarital affair can't instantly undo six years of close companionship. M and I still loved, even liked, each other. There was no hate between us. In some ways, that would have been much easier.

CHAPTER 2

THE BEGINNING

Neither of us had tried online dating before. But on January 1, eHarmony.com matched us as a potential couple. M was in New York. I was in L.A. She was about to cancel her membership but decided to stick around a little longer. I sent her a message the next day.

We spent the next three months talking on the phone and emailing. Though separated by a continent, we were as close as a tap of the keyboard. We wrote long emails to one another asking questions: *What's your favorite food? What makes you angry? If you could visit anywhere in the world, where would it be?*

She scheduled a visit to L.A. in March to interview for the graduate psychology program at Azusa Pacific University. It was the first time we'd meet in person.

I walked through the baggage claim doors at LAX and saw her sitting on the edge of the luggage carousel, in a blue Roots jacket with a red ball cap pulled over her face, talking on her cell phone. We caught each other's eye, she hung up, and we smiled. We hugged, I grabbed her suitcase, and we walked to my car.

In person, we hit it off instantly. We'd gotten to know so much about each other over the phone and email in the past few months, so we already felt comfortable with each other. On the way back from the airport, I took her to an amusement park where she beat me at air hockey.

Sitting in front of my bedroom bookshelf that night, we kissed for the first time. She interviewed the next day, gaining acceptance into the program at Azusa Pacific for the fall, and we knew she would be moving out to L.A. for sure now.

With her interview out of the way, we celebrated by hiking the dusty trail up Bronson Canyon to the Hollywood sign. Standing behind those iconic letters, gazing out over the sprawling L.A. basin, we kissed again. Her lips were soft and I could smell the sweat on her neck.

In April, I flew to upstate New York for a weekend to meet her parents. Nearly 30, we both had dated enough that we had a pretty good idea what we each wanted in a mate, and we told her mom and dad we were serious. We spent a day driving around looking at churches.

The Sunday evening before my flight back to California, we went to a Derek Webb concert outside Buffalo. After the concert, I proposed to her in the parking lot. The sky was streaked pink and scarlet. She said yes.

The rest of the summer passed in a blur of wedding preparation. We did marriage counseling with an old Baptist preacher who'd been a mentor of mine in college. Since M was in New York, I was in L.A., and Brother Ken was in Kentucky, we did our counseling sessions over the phone.

We covered all the potential trouble spots: sex, finances, role expectations, children. We were in that stage of the relationship where we were sure we'd see eye-to-eye on these big issues, and on the ones we didn't, our love would be enough to carry us through.

For our final session, M and I both flew to Kentucky to meet with Brother Ken in person. He looked at us and told told us he kept a handgun

14

in his closet. If his wife ever said she wanted a divorce, he'd go to the closet, get the pistol, and hand it to her. "You can kill me, but you can't divorce me," he'd say. He expected the same ironclad commitment from us. We were on board.

By August, we were standing at the altar of a small white Presbyterian church in the country outside Rochester, New York. We shared our vows before 100 friends and family members, kissed, then tugged on the worn rope in the vestibule that rang the old church bell announcing our union.

That night in our hotel room, she presented me with a leather-bound binder containing all of our e-mail correspondence since the date we were first matched. It was thick. She also gave me a smaller journal filled with handwritten notes from the previous year and a half. She penned these letters to her future husband. In them, she wished he could have met her late grandfather, asked forgiveness for past mistakes, and pledged her lifelong love to whoever received the book. I took it from her hands. I was the lucky one.

The next day, we packed our U-Haul trailer in her parents' driveway for our cross-country honeymoon drive to start our new life in California. M would be starting grad school and I'd be going back to pursuing my screenwriting career. M's father packed boxes and furniture, removed them, and repacked them in different configurations at least a dozen times.

He was stalling. He didn't want to see his little girl go. I couldn't wait to embark on our new life together. I can still see her parents growing smaller in our rearview mirror, watching as we drove away. I remembered a Rich Mullins lyric from a song at our wedding:

Just hold on tight
'cause it's a long wild ride
when you finally find the grace to love another as yourself

We buckled in and launched into the long wild ride, leaving behind our passionate whirlwind courtship for the promise of matrimony. But "finding the grace to love another as yourself" would not be as simple or easy. That, after all, is the work of marriage.

CHAPTER 3

BEAUTIFUL STRANGER

She's smiling in the photo, standing in a light blue summer dress beside the antique gas pump on Route 66 in New Mexico. We'd been driving for three days and were almost in California. I had to capture the image. She was luminous, and she was mine. I'd only known her for eight months, but I knew so much about her already.

She grew up in New York, an hour outside Niagara Falls. Her mother was half Mohawk Indian, from the Iroquois Nation, Turtle Clan. As a little girl, she sat on her front porch, asking strangers to be her friend.

She loved Pomeranians. After college, she was a social worker helping families adopt kids in Philadelphia. There, she got engaged to a decent guy, but broke it off after two years, when her gut told her he wasn't "the one."

She was highly intelligent and thoughtful. She suffered bouts of severe depression, and little orange pills saved her life. As long as she could remember, she'd been a Christian, a descendant of Mennonites who were themselves descendants of Old Order Amish. She grew up in church. Her faith was in her bones.

She was a reckless driver. Blondie's music got her moving. Injustice made her furious. Though she had a heart for the homeless, she recognized they were often mentally ill and dangerous. She could live on chicken Marsala and Girl Scout cookies.

I knew so much about her. And I had no idea who she was.

No matter how long or how well we've known the one we love, we always marry a stranger. We come to marriage as half-formed human beings, and that's if we're lucky. It's hard enough sometimes to understand ourselves, let alone another person. To complicate matters, we change as we get older. When M and I split up, she was not the same woman I'd met six years earlier, and I was not the same man.

You never solve the mystery of another person because the mystery keeps evolving. You never crack the code because the code keeps changing. That's just the way it is. And that's why it takes faith and a huge amount of courage to make a lifelong commitment to another person.

When times get hard or we get restless or the grass looks greener, we worry if we married the right person. But here's a secret: you never marry the right person. Because that person doesn't exist. You just marry another person willing to take the same leap of faith.

I could feel great affection for M, genuine love, and fierce loyalty. But even if she and I had stayed married for 50 years, I never would've fully known her. I don't believe that's the goal anyway. People aren't puzzles to solve. They're treasures to try to cherish.

So who was that girl in the blue dress standing beside the gas pump on Route 66 in the photo? She was my wife. She was a beautiful stranger.

CHAPTER 4

ALCATRAZ

After a few days in our new apartment, surrounded by open boxes and half-assembled furniture, we finally got around to opening our wedding gifts. Among the crystal bowls and china plates, I found a handwritten letter from my Uncle Tom, my dad's brother. I unfolded it and a $100 check fell out.

I set aside the check and read the letter. Uncle Tom wished me the best of luck. "I know you'll make the most of it," he wrote cryptically.

A Vietnam vet, Tom went on to compare marriage to a battlefield. But the analogies didn't stop there. "While some people describe marriage as a tropical island paradise," he wrote, "others compare it to another island altogether: Alcatraz."

The longer the letter got, the more brutal it became. I felt sorry for him. Who could blame him? He'd been divorced twice. His second marriage imploded in an acrimonious mess of custody disputes and alimony payments. He only knew what he knew.

M and I chuckled at the cynical letter. We knew that would never happen to us. Divorce had ripped through my family, claiming my parents, my mother's parents, my brother, and my uncles. But not me. I would be different. I was determined to break the cycle.

19

As a teenager, rooting around in the basement one day, I found a chunky, weathered photo album. On the cover was a black-and-white shot of my mother and father at the altar on their wedding day. The year was 1969. Seven years later, they'd be divorced.

Why did they split? What happened? I didn't know, and that day at age 14, I didn't care. I had more pressing matters, like how to smoke Camel Lights out my bedroom window without getting caught.

But I remember that photo. Dad, trim and fresh-faced. Mom, petite, pretty, beaming at his side. It was from another time, another world. The photo might as well have been taken on Jupiter. The two people in that picture were strangers to me. I had never known them like that: young or in love. I'm sure on that altar they never imagined getting divorced.

So how did my mother end up with the wedding photos years later? And why did she keep them? When M and I separated, I left our wedding album with her. I couldn't have held on to it. It would've been like holding on to a nest of fire ants. Maybe my father felt the same way, and that's how Mom ended up with their wedding photos.

I was a baby when my parents divorced. So I don't remember them as a couple. After they split, I lived with my mom while my brother Chad, four years older, went to live with my dad. One weekend, Chad would stay with Mom and I. The next weekend, I'd stay with him and Dad.

To my parents' great credit, they still took us to do activities together so we'd have a sense of who our family was, that we *were* a family, if fractured. They took us bowling, where Chad tugged on my shirt, causing me to slip in my socks and bust my front tooth on the slick floor. We went to a Harlem Globetrotters game, where one of the players kissed my dad on the lips to the stadium's great laughter. We went out for pizza.

20

Growing up, besides the occasional argument over a scheduling conflict, I rarely saw my parents fight. As far as I was concerned, they were just two people who loved me, but never two people who had once loved each other. Them being apart was all I knew, but I never gave any thought to what had pulled them apart.

Not until years later when faced with my own marital crisis did I start to speculate about what might have ended my parents' marriage. Vague reasons floated about over random conversations, pieced together in my mind: they were just too different, he wanted to travel the world with the Marines, she wanted to settle down and raise a family. But surely, it was more complicated than that. It always is.

A few months after M and I separated, I flew home to Kentucky for a month. I needed a change in environment. I needed to be around family. While eating at an old diner, my mom and I talked about divorce. Sitting at the counter, she turned to me on her red swivel stool. "I'm sorry Dad and I got divorced," she said. It wasn't a statement of regret. It was an apology.

It was okay, I said. I forgave her. Dad too. They were just two people who had tried their best, then had to pick up the pieces of their own broken dreams and expectations and move on. Just like I was going to have to do.

As far as I can tell, my parents' marriage was never like Alcatraz. It wasn't always Aruba either. It was somewhere in between. Just like mine.

CHAPTER 5

SPIDER WEB

No marriage—like no person—is ever all good or all bad. And mine had some shining moments. Still, looking back, the cracks showed early.

In the first years of our marriage, I worked as a substitute teacher to help pay the bills while M was toiling through grad school. We lived off my sporadic salary, her school loans, and the occasional loan from our parents.

M struggled between supporting my dream of becoming a working screenwriter and demanding that I do more to pay the bills. She'd get angry and resentful. We'd sit down and talk it out, and she'd express her frustration. I'd try to reassure her, and then we'd be good for another couple weeks. But the unspoken accusation ("You're not doing enough to provide") hung perpetually over us like a phantom. Even when we weren't talking about it, it was there.

More than once, she threatened to leave if things didn't change. This only made me anxious and resentful. On the altar, hadn't we committed to supporting each other even when times were hard? In my mind, I was doing all I could to provide. Difficult circumstances did not give her the right to threaten quitting the relationship. I needed to know she was my partner, not someone who might disappear on me.

Her depression didn't help. She could lose her temper and lash out at me when stressed. Aware of her sometimes-fragile emotional condition, I tried to be compassionate, but it wasn't always easy. I was trying my best to be a good husband, but her occasional volatility often put me on edge.

Two years into our marriage, I landed a full-time job as a copywriter and editor in the Office of University Relations at Azusa Pacific, the school M attended. I wrote radio spots, ad copy promoting academic programs, and features for the alumni magazine. I was grateful to have creative work and the people there became friends. Steady income started flowing in and some of the pressure on our marriage relaxed. The phantom retreated into the shadows. We could afford now to have a night out at a restaurant or go see a movie without worrying.

Still, the cracks remained.

Money wasn't the only issue. Early in our marriage, I expressed concern about her emotional ties to an ex-boyfriend. Just weeks before our wedding, she'd gone to his house and told him she was getting married and they had to cut off contact. They both cried. Even though they hadn't dated in a year, it felt like a break-up for both of them.

M confessed once that she thought of him occasionally and wanted to call him to see how he was. This set off alarms inside me. *Why does she still need to talk to him? Am I not enough?*

Their intimate relationship bothered me from the start. But since our courtship progressed so quickly, I never took the time to deal with my feelings of anxiety and resolve them. Instead, I pushed them down, assuming they would eventually evaporate as our marriage took hold. I was wrong.

We talked about this and she reassured me that I was in no danger of her cheating on me. After all, she chose me, not him. I believed her, and started seeing a psychologist to deal with my own emotional issues. The talk therapy helped a bit, revealing past traumas and explanations for why I might feel insecure. But the anxiety never fully lifted.

Around this time, a pervasive sadness began to grip me. Was it because of M's past connection with this man? Or was that just a symptom my mind had locked onto, starving for an explanation for my unease? Was it perhaps something much bigger than I even knew to consider?

The cracks were spreading.

I can mark the forceful onset of my depression to a weekend at Big Pine in Northern California, home to the John Muir national forest. In the 1890s, Muir, the famous explorer, ventured there to escape the din of modern life. In the 1930s, silent movie star Lon Cheney built a cabin in those woods to escape the klieg lights of Hollywood, preferring to quietly fish trout and spend quality time with his wife.

A group of men from my office had planned a weekend hike into the majestic peaks. On a Friday afternoon, we trudged in our gear up the craggy mountain trails. The higher we ascended, the more the snow covered the trees and brush until we were suddenly surrounded by crystalline white. It was everywhere. Immaculate. Pristine. Beautiful. And I felt a sadness so profound that I still lack the words to fully describe it. A sinister, alien grief invaded my chest and brain. But what was I grieving? The absence of M?

Just a few months earlier, M moved from California to start a yearlong graduate internship at Utah State University as part of her doctoral program. We flew back and forth to see each other every other weekend, but the separation, three years into our marriage, was hard. I missed her. Even so, a healthy mind should've been able to enjoy this bonding time with friends in nature.

We were steeped in rugged beauty. No pressure and no work deadlines, just a whole weekend to explore, laugh, and tell stories. Why was I so weighed down? What I felt wasn't the ordinary sadness of missing your beloved. It was too strong. Irrational.

After several hours of hiking, night descended, along with more heavy snow. We weren't even halfway up the mountain when the weather forced us to stop. We set up our tents in a clearing above an icy lake. We roasted Hebrew National dogs and slurped hot chocolate with bourbon by a small fire. We cracked jokes, jibed one another, and wondered what our wives were doing. Then we retreated into our tents.

I clicked on the small light attached to my headband and tried to read my dog-eared paperback copy of *The Little Flowers of Saint Francis*. Normally, this book edified me. But that night, something blocked me, an invisible membrane between the book and my mind. The words possessed no power to move or inspire. My brain struggled to make it through a few paragraphs. Finally, I put the book down and tried to sleep.

I awoke startled, engulfed in black. The tent wall had collapsed under the weight of a heavy snowdrift. I elbowed the snow off the tent, then scrambled to the entrance flap and flung it open. You could see the entire campsite by the moonlight reflecting off the snow.

I stepped out to get some air. Crunching across the snow, the sadness I'd been feeling turned into something like alarm, bordering on panic. I had the overwhelming urge to get off the mountain and back to the world. Back to familiarity.

I finally managed to sleep. When morning came, it was still snowing, so we decided it would be wise to cut our trip short and head back down to our cars. I was relieved. I never told anyone about my weird emotional experience on the mountain. But I knew it was not a good sign.

I was soon to learn that my own history with melancholy went much further back than that trip to Big Pine. It started before I was born.

One afternoon while driving through Studio City, my phone vibrated. It's illegal to talk on a cell phone while driving in California, but for some reason I answered it anyway. It was my mom, her tone unusually serious.

"Dad's in the hospital," she said. I whipped out of traffic onto the curb near a boxing supply store. Scenarios flashed through my mind. *Is it cancer? Did he drive his Saab off a cliff?*

"He's been sick for a while now," she said. "He has depression."

My father has always been positive, energetic, and gregarious. So to learn that he was depressed—to the point of being hospitalized—was disorienting. Apparently, he'd been talking to my mother for the past year about his darkening moods. Though divorced for more than 30 years, my dad still confided in my mom, and she still listened.

Over the past 12 months, Dad lost 30 pounds. The depression first hit him while he was stationed in Iraq. He considered stepping in the path of an oncoming Humvee. He worried about the nine millimeter Beretta strapped to his hip. It was too accessible.

Just as my father would do for me two years later, I immediately booked a cross-country flight to see him, with M's support. My mom and I drove to see him at the V.A. hospital, a brick building on an idyllic estate of rolling emerald hills and stately oak trees.

27

Eventually, the military doctors found a cocktail that rearranged the chemicals in his brain so that he could recognize the beauty of his surroundings again. Later, I learned my mom had suffered bouts of severe depression since her early twenties. Maybe I was genetically predisposed to inherit the condition.

Whatever the cause, I thank God that all of us—me, my mom and dad, and M—found medicine that worked to keep the black dog at bay. But for the longest time, I refused to try medication, seeing it as a weakness, a capitulation. To what, I'm not sure. The reality that men aren't as strong as we think we are? I had seen how medicine helped M's moods, so why was I so reluctant? Either way, the joke was on me.

You wouldn't tell a diabetic not to take insulin, and a person who's sick—in mind or body—is a fool not to receive an elixir that will manage his illness. So I eventually tried a variety of antidepressants until I found an effective concoction of Abilify, Zoloft, and Wellbutrin.

Two weeks after I started taking the pills, I woke up one morning, sat on the edge of my bed, and felt… normal. Not super-happy. Just not super-sad. Unfortunately, this relief finally happened just as our marriage was heading toward collapse.

One night, M and I went out for dinner. I noticed that one of the seven tiny diamonds had popped out of her engagement ring, leaving an empty socket. "We should get that fixed," I said. She agreed. We kept eating. We never replaced the diamond.

Around the time M returned from Utah, my career started to take off. A producer I'd been an assistant for years earlier contacted me to offer a job writing a cable TV movie. I submitted a sample script, took a few meetings with his creative partners, and was hired. I worked at Azusa Pacific during the day and wrote the script at night and on weekends.

Not long after I finished the first draft, I was accepted into the Warner Brothers TV Writers Workshop, a prestigious annual competition for aspiring writers. This led to a staff writing position on a drama for the FOX network. So I quit Azusa Pacific and went to work as a full-time TV writer. On the way out the door the first morning of my new job, I saw a note M left on the kitchen table, saying she was proud of me.

The show got cancelled after only six episodes, but working on it was a terrific experience. The other, more seasoned writers were supportive of my work, and I learned a lot. Fortuitously, only a month after the show's cancellation, I landed a gig on another show, an action drama on the Cartoon Network. This one lasted an entire 13-episode season.

I was doing what I loved and we were making more money than we'd ever seen. With our improved circumstances, it seemed our relationship finally hit a comfortable cruising altitude. But the cracks had never been fully sealed. Despite our improved financial situation, the fissures had splintered into a full-blown spider web, engulfing our fragile union. It would not hold up under the weight of what was coming.

CHAPTER 6

RETROUVAILLE

It means *renewal*. Retrouvaille is a Catholic-based organization that exists to help married couples on the verge of divorce. You don't have to be Catholic, or even religious, to take part. Volunteer couples host weekend seminars geared toward reconnecting you with your spouse, rediscovering the qualities that brought you together, and renewing your commitment to your marriage.

M and I had been together six years now, and lately she had been lamenting the lack of passion in our marriage. So when I learned of Retrouvaille on the Internet, I knew it was just what we needed. And they were hosting a weekend seminar near us in a month.

When I mentioned it to M, she was not nearly as enthused. This was discouraging. I couldn't figure out why she wasn't more supportive of attending the couple's retreat. After all, isn't that what she wanted? A husband who cared enough about the relationship to do whatever it took to keep it together? Despite her protests, I convinced her to join me on the upcoming weekend retreat.

We arrived at the hotel in Santa Clarita, an hour north of L.A., on a balmy Friday evening. As we got out of our SUV, a couple stood arguing in the parking lot. The woman stormed off, leaving the angry man frustrated. Apparently, we were in the right place.

In the lobby, two friendly women greeted us and handed us lanyards with our names. We checked into our room, then went to the first session. The hotel conference room drew together 15 struggling couples—young, middle-aged, and older. On a dais, a panel of three couples sat behind a long table and told us their stories. How they had met in hope, but then problems arose, affections deteriorated, and anger and despair took hold. Divorce seemed the only option.

Some experienced infidelity. Jason, a grown man, choked back tears as he told of cheating on his wife, Tina, who sat next to him. It wasn't an act. His pain and regret were sincere. Each couple had been to the brink of divorce, but with a lot of hard work, they each stepped back from that precipice and were now happy and strong.

One couple in their sixties stood out to me. Ed and Grace. They met in their late teens and she became pregnant. Her disappointed parents shunned Ed. Despite everyone's advice, they got married. Raising their first child at such a young age did nothing to strengthen their fragile relationship.

Ed began drinking. They argued daily. By their own admission, they despised each other. Eventually, Ed had an affair. They split up and lived apart for more than a year. Then more children arrived and they, too, were caught in the unhappy mess of Ed and Grace's failing marriage. But by some miracle, or an exhausted surrender, which is the same thing, they decided to try and salvage their marriage.

They began "dialoguing," they called it, sharing their thoughts in separate journals each night. Ed would write at least a page about what he was feeling that day—anger, hopelessness, gratitude—and Grace would do the same. Then they'd swap journals and read what the other had written.

After absorbing the other's innermost thoughts for a minute or two, they would simply talk about what they'd written, clarifying and expounding on their remarks. This typically led to further disclosures that opened each up to more intimate exchanges. Soon, they began to feel more compassion for one another. Compassion, understanding, and even affection again.

Ed and Grace's marriage had been a travesty. Who would have blamed them for throwing in the towel and trying to find happiness elsewhere? Their story gave me hope. After all, M and I didn't have half the problems they'd had. I wasn't a drunk, we weren't dragging any innocent children through our mess, and there was no infidelity (as far as I knew). If Ed and Grace could make it, then surely M and I had a chance.

In between the panel discussions that weekend, we split off to do our own "dialoguing." M went to the hotel room. I stayed in the conference room. We each wrote in our journals, tackling big questions. *What originally attracted you to one another? What is your greatest fear? Where do you hope to be in five years?*

After writing, I went back to the hotel room. We sat on the bed, read each other's journal entries, and shared our thoughts. We were instructed to set aside an hour for conversation. That seemed like a long time to talk, but the Retrouvaille panelists assured us that once we got going, an hour would be over before we knew it.

A couple times, M said she was just too tired to dialogue, so after reading my journal, she napped instead. I couldn't understand why she wasn't more into the exercise. What could be more important than working on our marriage?

In the sessions when the other couples shared their stories, though, M seemed invested. During one testimony, she leaned over and rested her head on my shoulder.

When Sunday came and it was time to leave, we were both emotionally exhausted. But I felt more hope than I had in a long time. Even the couple we'd seen arguing in the parking lot two days earlier had reconciled and decided to work on their marriage. "I feel good," I told M as we pulled away from the hotel. "Hopeful, y'know?"

"Yeah, we'll see…" she said. My heart sank. I hoped she'd been as affected by the weekend's events as I had. But it was almost like she'd already made up her mind that we weren't going to make it. Unbeknownst to me, she had. Her affair had already occurred.

After that weekend retreat, we started attending Saturday sessions at a nearby church to continue learning how to connect and heal our relationship. We listened to guest speakers—more couples who revived their faltering marriages—and did more dialogue exercises. These classes were less intensive versions of that first Retrouvaille weekend.

The panelists warned us that one weekend, however transformative, wouldn't save our marriage. We'd have to do the ongoing hard work that would repair the cracks and stabilize our union. That would take effort.

During this time, I got a phone call that the cable movie I'd written had finally secured financing and would be going into production in North Carolina in November, just a few weeks away. It was a big moment for me, the first time I'd be on set to see a crew bring my writing to life and watch actors perform my words. I wanted M to be part of this milestone. We'd make it into a vacation. It would be fun.

Once again, she was reluctant. But once again, she relented and booked a flight to join me, not for the whole shoot, but for a few days.

We had a good time in North Carolina. Between set visits, we hung out with some of M's local friends and visited historic downtown Winston-Salem, orange and gold and gorgeous in the fall. We explored the city, tried new restaurants, and dined with my father, who drove up from Kentucky to see us and watch the crew shoot a few scenes.

When it was time for M to fly back to L.A., I drove her to the small Winston-Salem airport. I'd be staying in town a few days longer. It was a wet, dreary day. I heaved M's suitcase out of the rental car trunk and set it on the curb.

"Kiss me," M said. I gave her a small kiss on the lips.

"No, a real one," she said. Our long kiss standing under the airport awning in the rain would be the last one like that. We separated, then she said goodbye, turned, and disappeared through the sliding glass doors. I got in the car and drove back to the film set under a drizzling, overcast sky.

A week later, she confessed her affair.

CHAPTER 7

EIGHT YEARS OLD

After the bomb dropped, we spent early December in a daze, like two shell-shocked victims stumbling through smoke and rubble. With Christmas approaching, we decided to spend the holidays apart. For the first time in our marriage, M went back East to be with her family while I traveled to Kentucky to be with mine. We agreed to not make any big decisions until we returned to California after New Year's.

I loved M, but I couldn't fathom staying together after what had happened. In my mind, a bridge had detonated and there was no way back across it. I didn't want to live a life where 20 years down the road, when things got hard or she got unhappy, another affair might be an option.

Even if I could work through the anger and betrayal, I couldn't bear living with that kind of uncertainty. So when we regrouped in January and she asked what I wanted to do, I told her I didn't see how we could get past this. She accepted it with little resistance beyond an obligatory "Are you sure?"

It seemed she wanted a fresh start—one without me. She said she was sorry for the affair and asked my forgiveness, but there were no desperate mea culpas, no all-out pleas to try and make it work. Instead, she offered to move out and live with her friend, Kathryn.

"You can stay here," I told her. "I'll find a place."

I didn't want to be left behind in the apartment where we'd shared so many memories. So that week, I drove an hour west to Burbank to look for a new home. If I was going to relocate, I wanted to be closer to the industry's movie studios and TV offices.

That first day driving around looking at apartments and houses was one of the most desolate of my life. I felt a chasm in my chest and my head pulsed with grief. I was on the razor's edge of tears from morning until evening. I wanted to be doing anything else.

After a few days, I found a quaint backhouse on a tree-lined street that felt like it could be home. That night, when M walked through the front door after work, I told her I had signed a lease. She stopped in the doorway, choking back tears. The split was becoming real.

Two Saturdays later, I sat on the floor in our guest room (where I'd started sleeping) sifting through files and knickknacks that I'd take with me when I moved into the new house. M sat on the bed watching me. Neither of us said much. In a box, I found my finisher's medals from several half-marathons we'd run together. I was going to throw them out, but she said I should keep them. Then she said something else.

"Who knows?" she said. "Maybe God can work a miracle and put us back together someday."

You can't just do whatever you want, then expect a miracle to bail us out, I thought. *You made a choice and that's why we're here. If you really wanted to save our marriage, you'd be making an effort now, not putting it off on God to fix later.*

It seemed she wanted to enjoy her "freedom" now, with the option of getting back together later, when *she* was ready. These thoughts, the anger, simmered, as I packed.

At the end of January, my friend, Dan (whose baby's baptism we attended the day M confessed her affair), showed up to help me move. While M was at work, we hauled my belongings out of the apartment and loaded them into a U-Haul truck. As we lugged out furniture, I kept our pug locked away in M's bedroom so she wouldn't dart outside.

Once everything was loaded, I let the dog out into the now-gutted apartment. She was oblivious, wagging her tail, happy to be free. I rubbed her head, gave her a kiss, and said goodbye. Then I locked the door and left the old apartment behind as Dan and I drove off. After six years of marriage, I was starting life as a single person again.

The new house smelled like fresh paint and waxed hardwood floors. That first evening, I stood in the living room, cavernous in its emptiness. There was no furniture, just the 50-inch flat-screen that M and I used to watch together.

We had few assets to split when we separated, but I ended up with the electronics: the TV, the Blu-ray player, the printer. Beyond that, I had a bed and desk, but no chair, so I sat lotus-style on the cold floor and watched a Redbox DVD.

After the movie, I shuffled to my bedroom and tried to sleep. It was my first night without M in the drafty new house with its unfamiliar noises. At midnight, a generator whirred to life outside my bedroom window, startling me. The walls buckled and popped as heat flooded the house. Everything was black. I lay there in bed, 35 years old. But I felt like I was eight.

When I was a kid, I stayed up late one night to watch a TV movie with my mom and her boyfriend. I still remember the title: *Testament*. In the film, a father leaves for work one morning, but a nuclear bomb drops, annihilating the town where he works.

His wife tries to contact him, but there's only silence. He never comes home. In his absence, she's left to raise their children alone. Her son (eight years old like me at the time) gets radiation poisoning. She tenderly washes him in the bathroom sink as dark blood spills from his orifices.

It was terrifying. How I ended up watching that much of it I don't know. But at some point, my mom sent me off to bed.

As I lay there, I could still hear the TV outside my bedroom door. I was paralyzed with anxiety. *The dad who never came back… the boy bleeding to death in his sink.* Though I couldn't articulate it then, that was one of the first times I realized that everything in the world is not okay. It's the same feeling I had lying in bed in my strange new house 27 years later.

CHAPTER 8

MADE OF ASH

I just wanted to sleep. But endless nights I lay there, tossing in my hot sheets, unable to drift off. The sadness was relentless. I thought about the stark fact that I'd never be with M again. It was over. Like death. This wasn't high school where we'd have a fight, then kiss and make up, or if we didn't make up, it didn't really matter because I'd forget her after a few weeks of adolescent angst, and carry on.

I wanted to wake up and have it all turn out to be a nightmare. But I knew it was real. The years would tick by until I died, and I'd never be with her again. Did I even want to go on living if this pain would never subside?

One night, as I lay in bed wrestling with these torments, I remembered M's "future husband" journal and the binder full of our emails she gave me on our wedding night. I'd taken them with me in the move. Throwing them out would have seemed almost like sacrilege, so they were stuffed away in my new garage, out of sight, but not out of mind, resting among boxes of books and old CDs. Suddenly, they seemed like something dead that had to be removed.

I got out of bed and walked across the small backyard to the garage. After finding the journal and binder, part of me wanted to open and read them again. But I resisted. What good would it do? It would only leave me in ruins, crying alone in my garage in the middle of the night. I decided I couldn't hold on to them any longer.

But what would I do with them? Burn them? I had a gas fire pit in the back yard, but it wasn't big enough to do the job, and I didn't want half-singed remnants of our love story stuck in a blackened pile. I could recycle them. But that didn't seem right either. There was always the off chance that a stranger might discover them in a bin and read them. I didn't want to risk that.

So I went in the house and dumped M's binder and "future husband" journal in a white plastic trash bag and cinched it tight. I tossed the trash bag in the passenger seat of my car and started driving. But where could I dump it? Anywhere I disposed of it would be forever tainted, like one of those makeshift memorials on the side of the highway, a wooden cross surrounded by flowers, a reminder of loss.

For lack of any better options, I drove a few miles to the second floor of a parking garage near downtown Burbank's restaurants and movie theater. This late, hardly any cars remained. Making sure no one was around, I dragged the trash bag out of my car and hoisted it into a public wastebasket near the elevator. I mashed it down so that it disappeared among the rest of the trash. Who'd ever find it there?

And that was that. Where did the journal and binder end up? My best guess: in a fetid landfill miles away in Sun Valley. But I didn't want to know. At least it wouldn't be haunting me from my garage anymore.

I walked back to my car and drove home. On the ride back, I fought to remain as still as possible. My whole body felt made of ash, and if I shifted ever so slightly, I'd crumble into nothing.

CHAPTER 9

PORTLAND

In the spring of my separation, I was offered a job writing a TV movie for NBC. I needed the work and happily accepted. The director lived in Portland, and the production company would fly me from L.A. to Oregon to meet with him, develop the story, and write a detailed outline for the script.

I booked a hotel room for a week. I flew to Portland, hoping that work on a new creative project would distract me from the ever-present sadness about my impending divorce. I arrived in the bright, crisp city, wet in April, and checked into my room downtown. I walked a few blocks to meet the film's director in his condo overlooking downtown's urban scramble. We got to work right away on coming up with the story.

At the end of that first day, I left his condo and walked the wet streets back to my hotel. I had my marching orders: take the ideas we'd talked about all day and shape them into some kind of narrative structure for the film. But when I got back to my hotel, all I could do was sit on the edge of my bed in the dim hotel room light. My mind tried to formulate ideas, but my heart kept interrupting. I deeply missed M. I felt like she should be there with me. This was not a convenient time for grief to strike.

I jotted a few ideas on note cards and tacked them to a corkboard. I stared at it. Then I crawled into bed, pulled the covers over my head, and shut my eyes. It was only 5 p.m. and soft evening light still streamed through the window. But I couldn't work. All I could manage was sleep. Not even sleep, just close my eyes and shut the world out. I didn't have the emotional energy to stay conscious, let alone the creative energy to develop a movie idea. As the hours crept by, the sun sank over Portland, darkness fell, and I slept the night away.

As the week wore on, I spent the days working on the movie idea with the director, and nights sitting in my hotel room wrestling with my grief. One night, the pain got so intense, I finally caved and called M. Part of me didn't want to—the prideful part that had been cheated on and felt she didn't deserve my surrender. But part of me couldn't help myself—the part that was devastated and missed my wife.

I told her that maybe we should consider trying to reconcile. Quiet hung on the other end. "Six years is a long time," she finally acknowledged. "We did invest a lot in our relationship. Let me think about it." We hung up. I felt no better.

When I returned to Burbank a few days later, I started writing the movie outline. But I was creatively barren. It wasn't normal writer's block. It was a crushing, overwhelming inability to concentrate and translate ideas into words on the page. With a fast approaching deadline and only a few rough pages, panic set in.

Sinking, I called my manager and told him I had to back out of the project. I just couldn't turn in a quality product by the deadline. My inner anguish consumed my mental and emotional energy. "Anguish" sounds dramatic, but it's not too strong a word for my experience.

Thankfully, my manager responded with compassion and made the call to the producers. I was relieved. But I had just given up a professional credit, a paycheck, and worst of all, I'd burned a bridge with my employers.

I wish I had been stronger that spring, four months into my separation, but I wasn't. *Emotional breakdown* had always been a removed, clinical term. Now I knew firsthand what one was like.

CHAPTER 10
DETOX

When an alcoholic quits drinking abruptly, his body rebels. It has become used to the drug over time and doesn't know how to live without it. His hands shake, his heart speeds up, he starts sweating, and he gets dizzy and agitated. Some people even hallucinate.

Why does this happen? Heavy, prolonged drinking disrupts the brain's neurotransmitters, increasing feelings of relaxation and suppressing excitability. But when you quit cold turkey, the neurotransmitters previously quelled by alcohol suddenly rebound, causing brain hyperexcitability that results in the withdrawal symptoms.

Abruptly quitting a person has the same effect. That's why a loved one's death can cause similar symptoms to alcohol detox. It affects us physically. We weep, heave, tremble, get disoriented and agitated. Some even hallucinate, seeing their lost loved one in the faces of passing strangers.

Divorce is very much like death. It *is* a death, of course—of love, a dream, a way of life, and so many other things. And like death, it forces us to cope with a sudden, devastating loss. M had been my wife for more than half a decade. I spent nearly every day with her for years. So when we split, she was still in my system. Learning to live without her would not be easy.

Quitting M instantly was too hard. So in the months after our separation, we continued to spend time together, not every day or even every week, but we'd meet occasionally for dinner or a movie. I would drive to the old apartment and visit our dog. We'd text or make sporadic phone calls, checking in on one another.

I wondered if this was healthy or if I just needed to cut off our communication completely in order to move on. Concerned, I spoke to my mom about it. She was understanding. She said if I felt like still seeing M, then I might as well just do it. There are no hard and fast rules for this kind of thing.

One place we met was the Pomona County courthouse. They offered free legal services to divorcing couples, helping them fill out and file the proper paperwork. The whole experience was a hassle and a nightmare of legal terms and forms that my brain had trouble wrapping around, so I was grateful for the assistance. But I also showed up to these meetings because it was an excuse to see M, even under such sad circumstances. I didn't have to; she could have filed the paperwork without me.

One morning every couple weeks, we met on the second floor of the courthouse and worked with a volunteer legal counselor (usually a student from a local law school) for a few hours, filling in information and signing forms. Then we'd leave and get lunch together. We'd eat burgers and laugh and catch each other up on our lives, as if nothing had changed.

But as comforting as it was to see her, it wasn't always pleasant. At one of the courthouse sessions, M grew frustrated and impatient with the process. She raised her voice, scraped back her chair, and stormed out of the room, leaving the other couples and volunteers staring awkwardly at me. Moments like that reminded me there were some things about our relationship I would not miss.

Every now and then, M would email to say she was near Burbank and ask if I wanted to grab a bite. I'd usually go. At one lunch, I noticed that she wasn't wearing her wedding and engagement rings. Maybe she was just getting them cleaned, I thought. I still wore mine. The way I saw it, we were still officially married and I intended to honor that commitment until dissolution. But the next time we met, her ring finger was bare again.

Another night a few weeks later, we met for dinner at a family-owned pizza pub we both liked. I nursed a beer while she sipped red wine. That night, just being there with her, sharing a pepperoni pizza at one of our old haunts, crushed me. I felt weighed down, draped in a lead blanket.

As she spoke, I stared at the table, struggling to concentrate. M asked what was wrong. I looked up, astonished. *What was wrong? Besides the fact that you had an affair, we're divorcing, and life as we know it has forever changed?*

I asked how she could be so nonchalant.

"I've just… accepted it," she said matter-of-factly.

I was stunned. I was crumbling inside and she had accepted it? Already? After only a few months? Accepted the end of our relationship, our marriage? Fighting tears, I turned my beer glass in a circle. The Pretenders' "I'll Stand By You" played over the pub radio.

CHAPTER 11

RUBICON

One summer afternoon, around seven months into our separation, everything changed. Still detoxing, I made a trip out to the old apartment to visit M and our pug. As we sat on the living room floor playing with the dog, M grew serious. She had something to tell me.

My stomach churned, just like the night she confessed her affair. I braced myself. Took a breath.

"Okay," I said.

She took another moment, then spoke.

"I'm pregnant."

My spirit sank. The revelation was so absurd, I didn't know whether to laugh or just get up and walk out. As I sat in bewildered silence, questions blitzed my brain. *Who's the father? Are you in a relationship? Was it planned?*

But as I sat there, it suddenly occurred to me: I didn't need the answers. It was none of my business now. I knew in that moment reconciliation would never happen.

It struck me, too, that I had apparently been holding on to a sliver of hope for us, even if I hadn't admitted it to myself. But with this news, the last embers of the burned bridge collapsed. I don't remember what else we said after that, but I left a few minutes later. What else was there to do?

The grief, anger, and rejection I'd been working through since we split were suddenly compounded. I was torn by conflicting emotions. I was furious, and yet I hated feeling angry with her because I was supposed to have loved and supported her. I wanted her to suffer, but I also wanted her to be okay. I was devastated that she could move on so quickly. Had I really been that expendable?

This raised questions for me about her very identity. Who was this woman? Was she this person who could sleep with another man before we were even divorced, and get pregnant? Is that who she'd been all along, and I just never saw it? Or was she the same woman capable of the close companionship, laughter, and warmth we'd shared for many years?

Was she basically a decent person who just got lonely and sad, making a rash decision in a moment of passion? Or did she have some deeper character flaw I had never detected? How had things gone so wrong?

Summer dissolved into autumn, and we kept in sporadic touch. One afternoon in October, I received a thick manila folder in the mail containing the final divorce paperwork. Eleven months after our separation, our marriage ended. A few days later, M stood before a judge who restored her maiden name.

Around this time, another envelope arrived in my mailbox. It was a five-page handwritten letter from M. She had just returned from a vacation to Greece with her friend, Kathryn.

M said she kept thinking it was me who should've been there with her, exploring ancient ruins and wading in the Mediterranean. She regretted her affair. She never should have listened to a priest who advised her to dissolve our marriage. She should have insisted we go to counseling. Was there any possibility I might take her back?

I set the letter on my bedroom desk, and pondered it over the next few days. Those pages contained the words I had longed to hear. But I needed to hear them months ago. By now, too much damage had been done. The letter arrived too late.

In November, almost one year after M confessed her affair, we got together to celebrate her birthday. Why not? We'd been together for her last six birthdays. It was tradition. We went out for brunch and saw a movie.

But something inside me switched that day. Unlike previous times we'd hung out since our separation, there was no sense of comfort in being with her. Instead, it felt wrong.

Too much had transpired and I knew we were never getting back together. Eventually, we'd both meet other people (apparently, she had a head start on that). Eventually, we'd move on with our separate lives. So why prolong the inevitable?

A couple weeks later, she emailed asking if I wanted to have lunch. I responded that we shouldn't see each other anymore. Too much had changed and we had different lives now. When I married her, it was to be my wife, not my buddy. When we married, I was all in. Now that we were divorced, I had to be all out.

A few days later, she responded by email. She said she hadn't stopped crying since she read my message. But she understood. She respected my decision. She ended saying she'd never forgive herself for hurting me.

I haven't seen her since, though we still speak on the rare occasion. But that day, we made the final, hard break. It was time to get on living life without her.

CHAPTER 12

CRUTCHES

Some people accuse religious believers of using God as a crutch. To which I reply, "Absolutely." Of course God is a crutch. There's nothing wrong with that. We all need crutches because we're all walking around on broken legs, especially during a trauma like divorce.

I've been a Christian since I was a teenager. Thankfully, during my divorce, I never felt like God abandoned me. I was often miserable and didn't understand why it was happening. But somehow, I always believed God was still real and present.

I tried to attend Mass every Sunday, even if all I could do was go through the motions and sit there feeling lonely. I knew it was important to be present. I needed to be reminded that God loved me in spite of my divorce, and who knew when I might hear a random Scripture verse or phrase in a homily that would buttress my sunken spirit or give me a scrap of hope.

There were hard nights when my anger flared at God. I wept and cussed and spit my prayers into what seemed like an indifferent void. I still believed in Him, but it was a messy belief, as belief usually is.

Some nights, I was too weary and bitter to pray at all. During those times, I simply offered up my silence as my prayer. I let my inability to pray *be* my prayer. And I knew that was okay. God would accept whatever I had to give, even if it was nothing.

I know not everyone believes in God. Faith is a gift I don't take for granted. I'm grateful to have it because I could not have gotten through my divorce without trusting that there was a God who cared about what was happening to me, that there might even be some good that could come from the wreckage, that my suffering might prove redemptive.

God was the most important crutch I leaned on to get me through my divorce. But He wasn't the only one.

The blue flames crackled from the fire pit in the backyard. My eyes followed the flames, twisting, dancing, vanishing in the dark. I cracked open another Miller Lite and gulped from the amber glass bottle. Was this my third? Or fourth? What did it matter? I just wanted to keep the buzz going. The lightness in my brain, the warmth spreading through my limbs.

I would not have said I was anesthetizing myself. I was just enjoying a six-pack on the patio. And I wasn't driving anywhere, so what did it matter?

When I ran out of beer, I turned to making Sidecars—brandy and Cointreau, with a splash of lemon juice. There's nothing wrong with enjoying a drink every now and then. But I had taken to enjoying more than a few most nights.

Before I knew it, I was using alcohol as a crutch. It made me feel better, for a few hours at a time anyway. It dulled my pain and took my mind off the dismal slog of my life. But it was a false solace.

Cocktails and light beers numbed me enough to keep me from feeling my heartache, but they wouldn't help me in the end, and if I relied on them too much, I knew they would only make matters worse. I was already a lonely divorcee. Did I really want to become a lonely, alcoholic divorcee?

Thankfully, I began to acknowledge (to myself if no one else) that I was drinking too much. I realized I used the alcohol to keep away the grief I actually needed to feel. If I kept blocking the pain, healing would never finally come. The pain and heartache and anger and despair needed to course through me so that healing could begin.

I cut back on the bottle. I had other, healthier crutches available.

I would not have made it through my divorce without my parents. Both my mom and dad listened when I needed to vent, get advice, or just know that someone loved and supported me. Mom was always just a phone call away. Dad flew out to visit me in Burbank on the first Thanksgiving following my divorce.

During that visit—the one-year anniversary of M's confession—not surprisingly, my depression struck again. Running out of my medication didn't help. Several mornings, I struggled to get out of bed. Dad ate breakfast, went for a jog, and read the paper while I slept until noon. He graciously allowed me the rest I needed.

As is our tradition, we went to see several movies over the holiday. Ironically, my depression lifted as we watched the film *Melancholia*. Sitting in the dark theater watching Kirsten Dunst's spot-on portrayal of a woman wracked with crippling despair, my own feelings of sadness gently dissipated.

Maybe it was seeing a character in my condition that reassured me I wasn't alone and lifted my spirits. Or maybe my refilled medication kicked in at that moment. Either way, when the lights came up, I could breathe again.

Besides my parents, I also had my friends.

Most of my close L.A. friends were married, some with children. They loved me, but they couldn't truly relate to what I was going through. This increased my isolation and loneliness. But fortunately, I had a couple buddies outside L.A. to whom I turned. Both men had been through divorce, and like me, had been cheated on by their wives.

Mike was a documentary producer in Omaha, Nebraska, whom I'd worked with years earlier. We touched base occasionally, but it had been at least two years since we'd last spoken. I knew he'd been through a heartrending divorce he didn't want, so I called him up.

Mike's advice and friendship became vital. No longer my former boss, he was now a friend, and just the one I needed at the time. I walked around the backyard, bare feet on the cool grass, chatting for hours on the phone with Mike. He listened to me and affirmed what I was enduring. He put words to what I was feeling. *Divorce rocks you to the core. You feel like a failure. You feel like a planet that's been knocked off its axis and now you're spinning out of control.*

Another crucial friend was William, back home in Kentucky. We graduated high school together and stayed in touch throughout the years. He was a groomsman in my wedding.

William caught his wife in an affair, also with a coworker. He struggled to get past it, and they tried to work through it, but a few months after the revelation, he learned she was still hanging out with the other guy.

One night, as she left the house for a company softball game wearing perfume, William told her that when she got back, there would be a "For Sale" sign in the front yard. Four months later, they were divorced. The day he moved into his new apartment, he sat down alone and sobbed for hours. Now this was a guy I could relate to.

Just having Mike and William to talk to, knowing they'd experienced what I was going through and survived it, gave me great comfort and strength. They were the lifelines I needed, setting the break inside me and allowing it to heal.

God. Booze. Family. Friends. Exercise. Music. Journaling. We all have different ways of coping with pain. Some work better than others, and some work against us.

Do what's good for you, toss out what isn't, but know that it's okay to use crutches. They help you heal. They'll help you keep shuffling forward, with misshapen bones perhaps, but forward nonetheless.

CHAPTER 13

STIGMA

Legend has it that in 1224, Francis Bernardone, who would become the famous saint of Assisi, received the *stigmata*. Mysteriously, holes appeared in his hands and feet, and his side was slit, mirroring the wounds of Christ. Francis' followers wrapped these bizarre supernatural wounds in bandages, but had to continually refresh them as the saint's wounds wouldn't stop bleeding until his death two years later.

Since then, others throughout history have reportedly received the same mystical wounds. Some devout Catholics see them as a divine gift, an intimate identification with the sufferings of Jesus. Others see the stigmata as something grotesque, the ghastly marks of a freak.

Stigmata, the plural form of the Latin word stigma, means "a mark of disgrace or infamy." And stigma is the right word for what we feel as divorcees. We walk around with an open wound that won't stop bleeding while horrified onlookers can't help but notice. Some feel pity for us. Some cross to the other side of the street to avoid us. Either way, we're marked.

About a year after my divorce, I went to a Christmas party. I walked through the door and a buddy approached with a glass of wine. "Hey, man! Where's your wife?" Matt bellowed.

"She's not my wife anymore," I said, trying to smile. A few other guests looked my way. The room quieted for a split second that felt like an hour. Matt's face dropped. "Ah… I'm sorry," he stammered. *Me too*, I thought. And just like that, I became the divorced guy at the party.

Matt, of course, didn't do anything wrong. He never intended to call me out publicly as the guy whose marriage didn't work out. How was he to know? He hadn't seen me in a year. He responded as graciously as he could and then we made awkward small talk, easing ourselves into more comfortable conversational territory. "So, still working in animation? How's the triathlon training going?"

And it's not just the annual holiday parties. It's everywhere you go where you might run into somebody who knew you as a couple. The grocery store. A birthday get-together. A swing by the old office to say hi to former coworkers. You're not safe anywhere.

A few months into our separation, I had a pitch meeting on the Warner Brothers studio lot. Afterward, I walked down the hall of the TV building to visit a producer friend. I sat on his plush couch.

"How's M?" he inevitably asked.

I didn't have the energy to get into our breakup. I was embarrassed and I didn't want to be a downer. So I lied. "She's good," I said.

"Is she still working as a psychologist?" he asked.

"Yep," I responded, then steered the conversation back to our favorite new TV shows. I didn't feel like being stigmatized that day.

The stigma makes you paranoid.

Your mind roils with self-conscious thoughts. You wonder what others are thinking. *What's wrong with him? Why couldn't he make his marriage work? How did he screw up?* Even if people aren't thinking those things, you feel like they are. You feel it like slits on your skin.

You feel it the next time you fill out a form at the doctor's office and check "Divorced" next to your marital status. You feel it when you subscribe to an online dating site and check "Divorced" as your relationship status, knowing that demoralizing category means a hundred options fall away because some people just don't want to date "damaged goods."

That's what you feel like now. And in a way, there's no denying it. That's what you are. You're unquestionably damaged. But damaged doesn't mean worthless. Damaged things can be fixed. Damaged things heal.

Still, the stigma's reach is long.

I sometimes teach TV writing for a Christian organization in Hollywood. In the thick of my divorce, a board member of this organization said that I should not be allowed to teach anymore because I was getting a divorce. Another board member spoke up and said that, on the contrary, that's exactly why I *should* be allowed to teach: because I was going through a hard time and needed community.

Another person took me to lunch and warned me that if I went through with my divorce, the Christian community in Hollywood would shun me. It was imperative that I make my marriage work. This person had no knowledge of my circumstances. He spoke as if it was as simple as me just deciding to stay together with my wife, as if she had no say in the matter.

Had he considered that maybe she didn't want that? That there were more factors at play than he knew about? No. He held to a black-and-white view of reality, while I was flailing in wretched gray.

But I get it. Divorce makes people uncomfortable. When we fail to live up to their idealistic standards, they chafe. I understand, and I try not to judge these people. They're disappointed and scandalized that you're not towing the line. They feel that somehow you're letting the whole tribe down by letting yourself and your spouse down.

But chances are these people have never been through what you're going through. Or if they have, perhaps they've never fully come to terms with their own failures and found peace with them. Everyone has their reasons, and the good news is that it's not up to you to figure them out.

Incidentally, the Christian community in Hollywood did not shun me. Almost uniformly, they loved and supported me without judgment. One older professional said that the problem with many Christians is that they think they have the answer before they've lived the questions. Most Christians I knew had lived their own questions so they did not condemn me. They bore their own marks.

The stigma was at its worst in that period after my split when I had to reveal to old acquaintances and close friends that I was getting divorced, like Matt at the Christmas party. But once I weathered those initial encounters, it got easier. The sense of shame lessened.

One day, three years later, I ran into an old high school classmate who never even knew I'd been married, let alone divorced. And that old paranoia flashed across my mind: *Does she think I'm a failure?* Only now, that negative thought receded as quickly as it came.

Because it had been long enough, and I'd come to know that I'm not defined by my divorce any more than by that job I lost after college or the arm I broke in third grade. I am not my wounds. Sure, they mark me. But they don't define me.

Divorce is part of my history, but it's not me. And so the stigma lost its strength as I became stronger. Divorce was a fire I didn't want. But in time, I began to emerge from the flames, burnt and better.

CHAPTER 14

THE THINGS WE LOSE

You may have heard the old joke: What happens when you play a country song in reverse? Answer: The guy gets his wife, home, dog, and truck back. My split was like a bad country song. I lost my wife, my home, my dog, even my truck.

A friend once said that what's most meaningful about his marriage was being able to look at the sky or a cathedral or a piece of art, to point it out and to have someone else there to see it too. Someone to behold with. In divorce, we lose that, and now we must look at the sky alone, without that other person to affirm us, to remind us we're alive by sharing the experience.

The first spring after my divorce, I started training for the Pasadena half marathon. Running up to five miles a day was a good way to clear my mind and boost my mood. M and I used to train for races together. We'd strap on our running shoes, set our iPods to record our distance, then take off, jogging the neighborhood sidewalks under leafy sycamore canopies. After a few minutes, I'd pull ahead of M. At the halfway point, I'd turn back around to complete the loop. M was never too far behind, and we always high-fived as we crossed each other on my way back. Running was good for us.

After we split, running didn't remind me of her. It was something I could still do solo and feel good doing. But a strange thing happened as I crossed the finish line at the Pasadena half marathon. Instead of feeling the sense of elated accomplishment familiar to race finishers, my first instinct was to look into the crowd for someone to hug and celebrate with. But she wasn't there.

I slowed to a trot, ambled through the crush of people, received my finisher's medal, and swigged some water. I distinctly remember missing M at that moment. Normally, she would have been in the crowd to greet me with a sweaty hug, and we'd mill about the race expo together before walking back to our vehicle, stiff, sore, and content.

Training for the race had not reminded me of M. But at the finish line, I suddenly wanted her there. My cheerleader was gone.

And my spouse wasn't the only one I lost. For six years, I had another family: M's mother and father, her brother and sister-in-law, and my two little nieces. Whether you get along with your in-laws or not, they become a part of you, woven into your thoughts, emotions, and history. Suddenly, they're forced to choose sides. Naturally, they choose their blood, though they may sympathize with you. And there goes half your family.

Mutual friends divide too.

I am fortunate to have a core group of friends I've known for years. They stood firmly in my corner during my divorce. But there are other friends and acquaintances you make as a couple: M's fellow graduate students, my coworkers, couples at church. So who gets Debbie in the breakup? Who gets Greg? Now, these people must choose which person deserves their loyalty. For some, the decision is easy. For others, it hurts. Many mutual friends liked us both equally and they didn't ask to choose between M and me. The collateral damage of a divorce is real, and other people lose as well.

And it's not just people. I lost places.

During our marriage, M and I lived in three different towns, but all part of the same general community. We got to know the local Albertson's grocery store, the dirt-patched dog park, the small downtown with its corner pastry shop, and the hiking trails at the base of the foothills. These places formed our home.

After we separated, I moved to Burbank, an hour away. But for a couple months, I occasionally drove back to the old neighborhood. Not to spy on M, but just to drive around the same familiar streets I'd enjoyed for so long.

There was the local Italian restaurant where we ate brunch buffet every Sunday morning. After the split, we met there to discuss the details of our impending divorce, but we still enjoyed the ambiance, the bruschetta and penne alla vodka, the champagne, and the jolly, stocky waiter who sang happy birthday to patrons. This special place of ours was hard to let go.

The last time we had dinner there, we stood up from our booth to leave and noticed an older couple looking at us. The lady smiled. "You are such a sweet-looking couple," she said. We thanked her, paid our bill, and drove to our separate homes.

Occasionally during our marriage, we took weekend road trips from L.A. to Zion National Park in southern Utah. We hiked the red rock canyons and soaked in the rugged beauty of the prehistoric rock formations, hidden waterfalls, and coral pink sands. We felt close in Zion. The geography seemed to strengthen our bond.

A while ago, M asked if I've been back to Zion since we split. I haven't. It's still breathtakingly beautiful, its majesty indifferent to the trials and tragedies of the countless people who've passed through there. But if I went back, all that beauty would hold a pervasive sadness, like thick summer heat trapped in the canyon air. I didn't just lose my wife in my divorce. I lost Zion too.

Along with places and people, divorce takes away dreams.

I had a dream: that I'd be a happy man in a successful marriage. Now that's gone. I dreamed I would be a father, tossing football in the front yard and hosting princess parties out back.

M and I tried to have kids, three times, but it didn't work. Now I'm grateful, only because we didn't have to drag innocents through a breakup they didn't ask for or deserve. Maybe you've had to haul your children through a toxic separation. Or maybe, like me, you've lost the dream of possibly being a parent. Time waits for no one and now I'm single again with the clock ticking faster each day.

Maybe one day, I'll get remarried and have children. My Uncle Tom ("Alcatraz") was 52 when he had his first of two kids. Maybe that's in the cards for me. Maybe not. All you can do is take it one day at a time.

The dream of being a strong husband. A good father. A respectable man with a burnished band on his left hand. The dream of maybe sitting in rocking chairs on a front porch somewhere, grown kids visiting, me and my beloved frail but together after a lifetime, holding one another's withered hands. All gone now.

But perhaps the greatest loss of all in a divorce is the sense of self. Marriage makes a huge imprint on a person's identity. In marriage, I wasn't just Chris anymore. I was a married man. I was M's husband. I was Lilly and Maggie's uncle.

Then suddenly, I was not.

Divorce scrambled my identity. Who I thought I was—a man who could marry and be happy and stable—was violently sucked into a vortex with no definitions. I was plunged into a blackness, without gravity, frigid and infinite. And I drifted there, unmoored.

But there's a flipside to losing so much: I also started to find.

I found who I never knew I was: a man strong enough to withstand all this loss. My heart was still beating, still full of potential coiled to burst forth into the world.

During my divorce, I often felt as if I had nothing left. But from the dregs of nothing, something sprang forth. And in time, I discovered that I still had it in me to live, to try to love. I may not have felt it in the thick of every lost thing. But it was there, waiting to happen.

CHAPTER 15

RESURFACING

There's a steel bridge in my hometown that hums when cars traverse it. They call it the singing bridge. It stands above the Kentucky River that bisects downtown Frankfort.

When I was young, I had a recurring dream that I was falling backward off that bridge. My heart raced and fear flooded my veins. But once I hit the water and sank beneath the surface… I could still breathe. So suddenly I wasn't afraid, just suspended underwater, looking up at the bottom of the bridge, rippling and shimmering above the surface.

That's what it's like to lose a marriage. You fall from safety. You can't control the drop. You're petrified. All seems lost. You plunge into a murky new world. The water is heavy. Strange creatures swarm about. You don't know where the bottom is. You're a mammal with lungs suddenly suspended in an environment that requires gills to survive. And yet… somehow you can still breathe. So you don't have to be afraid.

You *will* be afraid. But you don't *have* to be.

You'll never be the person you were before you fell from the bridge, in those days when you were dry and safe and the hidden world below was just a rumor. Now you know it exists and there's no denying that dark reality.

Eventually, you resurface. You suck oxygen into your lungs again and it feels natural, like riding a bike they say, something your muscle memory never forgot how to do. You swim to shore, crawl through the sludge, and step onto dry land.

You look around and you have resurfaced to find that the world is different from how you remembered it. It may look the same. But you know the deeps exist now and they have forever changed you.

The first woman I dated after M was Sarah, an attorney who lived an hour away. I met her online. We met for sushi. We saw a scary movie. We met for a second date. We talked on the phone for hours at a time. It was nice. I missed female companionship. Eventually, our phone calls became less frequent. We sent the occasional text. And then… that was it.

Losing touch with Sarah didn't feel like a big loss. After all, she wasn't M.

In truth, I felt perfectly comfortable sitting across the table from a new woman, sharing a martini under dim lighting. I enjoyed cowering and laughing together over popcorn at scary moments in a dark movie theater. It wasn't hard or awkward. But it wasn't the same as sharing a moment with the one who's been your best friend for six years. However diverting it might have been, my heart wasn't in it.

I met a few other women online and through mutual friends who set me up on blind dates. Again, we met for drinks and appetizers. We saw movies and chatted on Facebook.

And it was a weird conundrum. Early in my separation, while I was still married, I was at my loneliest, so I wanted to be with someone. But it was M I wanted to be with.

I was tired and didn't have the emotional energy to build memories with someone else. I liked the memories I had with M. I wanted to build on those.

I was still grieving the loss of my wife and the life we'd built together. I was in no shape to be dating again. Not yet. It wouldn't be fair to any woman who might take a real interest in me. I just wasn't available.

I could've gone another route: enjoy my newfound "freedom," meet a variety of new women, and have a lot of sex. I deserved it, right? I even needed it. Especially at a time like this. I needed the warmth, the physicality, the connection to another person. One could make that argument.

But no one needed to tell me that this path, with its pleasures, also brought its perils. Did I really want to get tangled up with someone new when I hadn't yet made peace with my failed marriage? Also, because of my faith, this wasn't an option I allowed myself.

Perhaps not an option, but definitely a possibility. I'm as red-blooded and vulnerable as the next guy, and I'm not immune to sexual lures. My history had proven that. But I knew that any emotional connection would have been bogus, any sexual encounter hollow, ultimately more harmful than rewarding.

Besides, resurfacing isn't about diving right back in to another relationship with a more-than-better chance of ending in disappointment for both parties. If my brief courtship and divorce taught me anything, it taught me to take things slow. We are all desperate for love, but real love comes slowly, not at first sight.

So when will you know you're ready to date again?

The answer differs for every person. Healing follows no fixed timeline. Take care of yourself first. My friend, William, gave me some great advice. He said if there is ever a time to focus on *you*, it's during a divorce. You have to make sure you're healthy before embarking on another relationship.

I know one thing. If and when I find someone new, I won't count on passionate feelings or butterflies to confirm that she's "the one." I don't believe in soul mates anymore. I believe in beautiful strangers. I believe that we're called to do our best to love others, and if we're fortunate enough to have that *other* be part of a romantic relationship, then we should relish it while expecting the inevitable challenges that loving another fallible person brings.

If soul mates existed, we'd be screwed. Because if we met our one cosmically exclusive mate, but something went wrong and we were separated from them, then the romantics would be right: we would truly have no need to go on living. But it happens all the time, and we go on.

We humans are resilient creatures. We're made to love, yes. But we're also made to bounce back from failed love. I've learned that. We're made to keep loving, to keep hoping. We fall, but we keep falling forward.

CHAPTER 16

MOUNTAINTOP

I trudged up the dirt trail, my quads burning from the effort. It was the first week of autumn and a mild breeze blew occasionally across the path, drying my sweat. Garcia Trail is a jagged course of switchbacks that ascends a mile skyward to a point overlooking Azusa and its surrounding towns. On a clear day, you can see all the way to Pasadena almost 13 miles to the west. The last time I'd tackled this trail was with M. Today, I climbed alone, except for a few hikers who passed me on their way back down. We nodded our hellos and continued on our separate paths.

After 45 minutes, I reached the top and sat down to catch my breath. Nearby, two crude wooden beams stood nailed together in the shape of a cross, towering 10 feet toward the sky. Students from Azusa Pacific University planted the cross here years ago. A metal box lay at its base, with a lid that swung open to reveal a weathered green spiral-bound notebook. Climbers could jot down their names, proving they were here, and scribble prayer requests for others who might find the notebook after them.

I walked over to the cross and pulled a trowel from my Camelback. Then I knelt down, cracking the hard earth with the spade. I dug through the dirt and rocks, scooping out a hole. Then I reached in my pocket and withdrew my wedding ring.

I'd heard a wide range of opinions on what to do with my ring after my divorce. Some said I should pawn it for cash. Others suggested dropping it in a church's offertory box as a gift. I imagined going to Malibu, where M and I made out on the beach one night, and hurling the ring into the surf. But none of these options seemed right.

Despite all that had happened, I still saw my marriage as sacred and this bright little band represented that covenant. So I would leave it up here at the Garcia Trail summit, at the foot of the cross, a place of death, but also new life.

I set the ring in the ground and covered it with dirt. I patted down the loose soil, and got to my feet, standing beside the cross and gazing out at the valley below.

Glendora glimmered in the distance, the town where M and I moved into our first cramped one-bedroom after we married. I glanced eastward and saw the community of Azusa, where we moved to our next apartment because it allowed dogs. Further south, I recognized San Dimas, the last place we lived in the final years of our union. From this vantage point, I could see all these towns, the places where my marriage had lived and died.

Eight years ago, we had met in hope and excitement. Now here I was, burying my wedding band in the dirt. I thought of how sad it is that things which begin with such joy and promise can end so disastrously. I realized that this day, two years after my marriage imploded, I still had no definitive answers for why things ended up the way they did. Answers would come, emerging as they do in bits and pieces from the insight that time brings.

But at this point, I was sure of one thing: I had survived. Though I would still have bad days and tears left to shed, the worst was over. I was going to make it.

All these thoughts swirled in my head as the breeze swept around me. It was peaceful up here. Tranquil. The wind smelled of dirt and sage. I had done what I came to do. I had buried the dead. I took one last look at the patchwork of towns below, then I turned around and made my way back down the trail, back into the land of the living.

CHAPTER 17

TAKING OWNERSHIP

It's never just one thing or one person that explodes a marriage. It's a messy and confusing conflagration of events, circumstances, and choices on the part of both parties. Usually, you can't even start to see everything that wrecked it until the smoke clears, and that can take a long time.

It would be easy for me to blame my marriage's failure solely on M's affair. It would be simple and clean. But it wouldn't be accurate.

The only way to inch toward peace—with your ex-spouse and with yourself—is to own your contributions to the marriage's failure.

I sometimes prioritized my career over M when I should have reassured her she was the most important thing in my life. I said things that hurt her, words I wish I could take back. When I was depressed, I sometimes directed my anger and sadness at her when she had nothing to do with it.

Also, we never tried couples therapy, neither during our marriage nor our separation. Would it have made a difference? There's no way to know. Even if counseling wouldn't have ultimately kept us together, it might have enlightened us as to all that went wrong so we could each dodge the same landmines in future relationships.

Another mistake we made is moving too fast when we first met. We were in love, slaves to our future dreams and endorphins, and all we wanted was to be together. That's fine. But we had known each other for less than a year when we made our vows. We would have benefited from taking more time to get to know each other.

Does that mean we never should have gotten married at all? That the whole thing was a mistake? Again, there's no way to say for sure.

If I had it to do over again, would I do some things differently? Yes. And yet, I don't regret being married to M.

That sounds like a contradiction, I know, but it's not. Love is not math or science. It doesn't always add up, and you can't dissect it in a lab to see how it works. It lives in the realm of mystery and paradox. That's what makes it tricky and that's what makes it awesome.

Some would say that if your marriage ends in divorce, then all those years you spent with your ex amount to a loss. But I emphatically refute that. Those years are not lost. For one, those years inevitably held some good. But also, every painful moment bore a lesson that will make you stronger in the future.

My years with M were some of the hardest and the most sublime of my life. And isn't that what life is anyway? A continuous ebb and flow between peace and turmoil, laughter and tears, good times and bad? I'm grateful I lived it out with her for a season.

At the same time, I have to be honest: I made mistakes, yes, but I cannot bear all the blame for how things turned out. Though it would take me a while, I eventually concluded that I'll never fully know why M had her affair, and then had another encounter that resulted in bearing a child who wasn't mine. Sure, I could point to the usual suspects: depression, loneliness, discontent.

But as compassionate as I want to be toward M, I also have to acknowledge that she's an adult who made her own decisions. Countless couples experience seasons of unhappiness and even despair, but they stay faithful to their vows. Ultimately, only M is responsible for her choices. And though far from the ideal man, I feel peace knowing that I genuinely tried to be a faithful and good husband throughout the years.

So I stopped trying to understand why M did the things she did. A person could go crazy trying to make sense of it. I also chose to stop bearing the burden of guilt over it all. I own my mistakes, and I will try to do better in the future. That's all I can do. I hope M does the same.

I haven't seen her in years. We still text and chat occasionally, punctuated by long stretches of no communication in which we're each busy living our new lives. I pray for her and wish her the best. There was a period when I didn't feel that way, when I was too consumed with anger and bitterness to wish her well. That time has passed.

Just the other day, three years after our divorce, I was sifting through a box looking for a book, and I came across a tiny wood-framed photo that had been tucked away and forgotten. There we were, smiling in a park while visiting M's brother in Philadelphia. We were content, happy, unaware of what the future would bring. I studied the photo, remembering that moment, remembering those better days.

Suddenly seeing M's smiling face in a photo, us together, caught me off guard. I felt a pang of sadness. But now… it was different. It wasn't the white-hot anguish of the early days of my divorce. It was a soft gray, an overcast sky, a cool October storm. And like a storm, the feeling rolled in, then quickly dissipated.

And that's when I knew more healing had happened. I didn't have the urge to burn the photo or stuff it in the trash. I glanced at it, felt poignant, then moved on.

That's how healing happens, and how peace comes. Not all at once, as we wish they would, but gradually, quietly, over the span of years. But they do come. I glanced at the photo one last time, then tucked it back in the box and kept looking for my book.

EPILOGUE
PHANTOM PAINS

I'm driving down the freeway, letting my left arm dangle out the window. I like the feeling of the breeze whipping against it. And then—instinctively—I clench my fingers into a fist because I'm afraid my wedding ring will slip off and go clinking down the road. Then I remember: I'm not wearing my wedding ring. I haven't for at least three years. And yet, I can still feel it. Physically.

It brings me back to my wedding day. I remember looking at my new wedding band as I gripped the steering wheel while pulling out of the church parking lot. "It feels strange," I said. My father smiled. "Get used to it," he replied. And I did.

Over the years, it became another part of my body, physically inseparable from who I was, like my brown eyes or my arms and feet. It reminded me that I was now joined to M, and she and I had become one flesh. The ring bonded with my skin to remind me, and others, of this reality.

Years went by. My wife and I made love and argued and cried and wondered how we'd pay bills. We suffered miscarriages. We pulled through. We were young and we learned as we went. And through it all, that titanium ring clung to my finger, an anchor holding me in place even

83

as life circumstances threatened to rip our union apart. I was proud to wear it. It made me feel special. It made me feel connected to another person through every trial and celebration. It was part of me.

One anniversary, we went snorkeling in the Pacific. My fingers shrunk in the cold water, and my ring slid off. I swiftly clenched my fist and barely saved it from sinking. A close call, but I clung to it tightly and swam the rest of the day with my left hand balled into a fist. I was not going to lose that ring. And I never did.

Then one night, M sat me down on the couch and made the confession that shattered our marriage. We split up. I moved out and found a new place. We started our divorce paperwork. But I still wore the ring. It was still too much a part of me, and the way I saw it, we were still married.

A few months before the divorce became official, I finally removed the ring. For weeks, it rested on my nightstand. Then I placed it in a desk drawer where I couldn't see it, where I wouldn't constantly be reminded of it. Gradually, the pale line and indentation on my ring finger faded and it looked as if I'd never worn it.

But then one day after the divorce, it happened. I was driving and I felt—physically felt—the ring on my finger. I clenched my fist to protect it, but then realized, of course, that it wasn't there anymore.

Medical professionals call this "phantom pain." Often, when someone loses a limb or other body part, the body still "feels" the appendage as if it had never been removed. Missing feet itch. Missing knees bend. Missing hands grasp.

American neurologist Silas Weir Mitchell described the phenomenon of "spirit limbs… haunting soldiers." Occasionally, I still feel my wedding ring. Not always. But from time to time, it "haunts" me.

Maybe it always will. Or maybe one day, I'll get married again and the sensations will go away. I'm not sure. It's all a mystery, just like most things involving the body and mind and soul.

But I believe the pain can be good. Every time I "feel" that ring, it's like a holy reminder that I lost something precious, a once-vital part of myself that will always be missing now. And that's okay. Because that just reminds me that I'm alive and I'm capable of feeling and loving. And healing.

And as I think about it, I suspect that the path to healing involves loosening my grip. When I drive down the road, I may occasionally feel that phantom wedding band slipping off my finger. But I don't need to clench my fist tight anymore. I'm not going to lose the ring. The ring is gone. I just need to let it go. The future is ahead.